Geology Zone

Fossils

by Julie Murray

Dash!
LEVELED READERS
An Imprint of Abdo Zoom • abdobooks.com

Level 1 – Beginning
Short and simple sentences with familiar words or patterns for children who are beginning to understand how letters and sounds go together.

Level 2 – Emerging
Longer words and sentences with more complex language patterns for readers who are practicing common words and letter sounds.

Level 3 – Transitional
More developed language and vocabulary for readers who are becoming more independent.

abdobooks.com

Published by Abdo Zoom, a division of ABDO, PO Box 398166, Minneapolis, Minnesota 55439.

Printed in the United States of America, North Mankato, Minnesota.
102024
012025

Photo Credits: Shutterstock
Production Contributors: Kenny Abdo, Jennie Forsberg, Grace Hansen, John Hansen
Design Contributors: Candice Keimig, Neil Klinepier

Library of Congress Control Number: 2024936538

Publisher's Cataloging in Publication Data

Names: Murray, Julie, author.
Title: Fossils / by Julie Murray
Description: Minneapolis, Minnesota : Abdo Zoom, 2025 | Series: Geology zone | Includes online resources and index.
Identifiers: ISBN 9781098287153 (lib. bdg.) | ISBN 9781098287856 (ebook) | ISBN 9781098288204 (Read-to-me ebook)
Subjects: LCSH: Fossils--Juvenile literature. | Rocks--Identification--Juvenile literature. | Geology--Juvenile literature. | Earth sciences--Juvenile literature. | Paleontology--Juvenile literature.
Classification: DDC 560--dc23

Table of Contents

Fossils

A fossil is the remains or **trace** of something that lived long ago. These remains are preserved in rock. They can be anything from bones to footprints and shells.

Not all living things become fossils. Most dead **organisms** are eaten or rot away. Usually, only the hard tissue remaining becomes a fossil.

Fossils are formed when **sediment** covers a dead **organism**. The sediment can be dirt, sand, or even volcanic ash. Then, the soft tissue **decomposes**. The hard parts, such as bones, are left behind.

Over time, more layers of **sediment** build up. This causes great pressure. Eventually, the layers harden into rock. This process forms a fossil.

11

Kinds of Fossils

A body fossil is the preserved remains of an animal or plant. It can be the entire **organism** or just part of it. Bones, teeth, and leaves are all examples of body fossils.

Mold and cast fossils are types of body fossils. A mold is an imprint left by an **organism**. A cast forms when the imprint fills with **sediment**.

A **trace** fossil is anything left behind that was made by an **organism**. This can be a footprint, burrow, or even dung. Trace fossils show an organism's behavior.

Finding Fossils

Erosion often exposes fossils. Scientists also look for fossils in certain areas. They use special tools to **excavate** fossils.

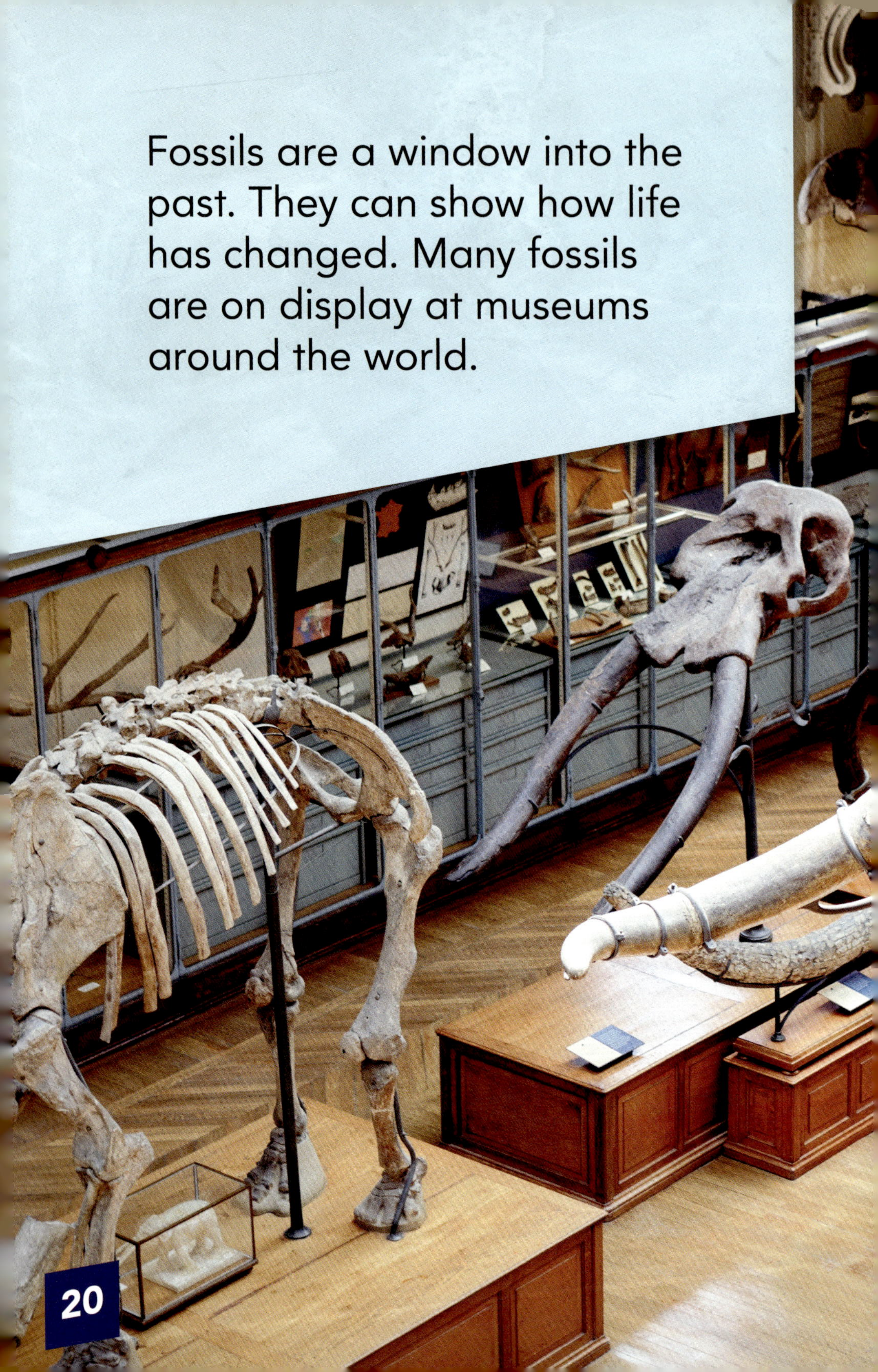

Fossils are a window into the past. They can show how life has changed. Many fossils are on display at museums around the world.

More Facts

- The word fossil comes from the Latin word *fossilis*. It means "dug up."
- The oldest known fossil is 3.5 billion years old! It is a blue-green algae found in Western Australia.
- Fossilization can take anywhere from days to tens of thousands of years.

Glossary

decompose – to decay.

erosion – the wearing away of the earth's surface by wind or water.

excavate – to uncover by digging.

organism – an individual living thing, such as a plant or animal.

sediment – small pieces of solid matter that settle at the bottom of a body of water.

trace – a mark or sign of a past event or thing, such as nests, footprints, and dung.

Index

Online Resources

To learn more about fossils, please visit **abdobooklinks.com** or scan this QR code. These links are routinely monitored and updated to provide the most current information available.